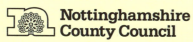 Nottinghamshire County Council

Please return / renew by the last date shown.

Animal Body Parts

Amphibian Body Parts

Clare Lewis

a Capstone company — publishers for children

Raintree is an imprint of Capstone Global Library Limited, a company incorporated in England and Wales having its registered office at 7 Pilgrim Street, London, EC4V 6LB – Registered company number: 6695582

www.raintree.co.uk
myorders@raintree.co.uk

Text © Capstone Global Library Limited 2016
The moral rights of the proprietor have been asserted.

All rights reserved. No part of this publication may be reproduced in any form or by any means (including photocopying or storing it in any medium by electronic means and whether or not transiently or incidentally to some other use of this publication) without the written permission of the copyright owner, except in accordance with the provisions of the Copyright, Designs and Patents Act 1988 or under the terms of a licence issued by the Copyright Licensing Agency, Saffron House, 6–10 Kirby Street, London EC1N 8TS (www.cla.co.uk). Applications for the copyright owner's written permission should be addressed to the publisher.

Edited by Helen Cox Cannons and Shelly Lyons
Designed by Steve Mead
Picture research by Svetlana Zhurkin
Production by Victoria Fitzgerald
Originated by Capstone Global Library Ltd
Printed and bound in China

ISBN 978 1 406 29805 5
19 18 17 16 15
10 9 8 7 6 5 4 3 2 1

British Library Cataloguing in Publication Data
A full catalogue record for this book is available from the British Library.

Nottinghamshire Education Library Service	
E220105247	
Askews & Holts	Sep-2015
597.8	£11.99

Acknowledgements
We would like to thank the following for permission to reproduce photographs: Alamy: Barrie Watts, 21, 23, Natural Visions, 22 (middle); Dreamstime: Chris Moncrieff, 8, Jozsef Szasz-fabian, 15, Mikelane45, 5; Getty Images: Dante Fenolio, 18, Joseph T. Collins, 17, Michael Langford, 19; iStockphoto: Snowleopard1, back cover (left), 7; Minden Pictures: Pete Oxford, 22 (bottom); Newscom: Photoshot/NHPA/Stephen Dalton, 12; Shutterstock: Alfredo Maiquez, 4, assistant, 23 (bubbles), Chris Hill, 22 (top), Don Mammoser, 6, 23, Dr. Morley Read, cover (top left, top middle), Eric Isselee, cover (top right), Hugh Lansdown, 23 (two frogs), Ilias Strachinis, 10, Jason Steel, 13, Johan Larson, 14, Peter Baxter, 20, Sebastian Duda, cover (bottom), Tony Campbell, back cover (right), 11, 23, WitR, 16, Wong Hock Weng, 23 (fly); SuperStock: Rauschenbach/Mauritius, 9.

We would like to thank Michael Bright for his invaluable help in the preparation of this book.

Every effort has been made to contact copyright holders of material reproduced in this book. Any omissions will be rectified in subsequent printings if notice is given to the publisher.

All the internet addresses (URLs) given in this book were valid at the time of going to press. However, due to the dynamic nature of the internet, some addresses may have changed, or sites may have changed or ceased to exist since publication. While the author and publisher regret any inconvenience this may cause readers, no responsibility for any such changes can be accepted by either the author or the publisher.

Contents

What is an amphibian?......................**4**
Eyes **6**
Teeth and tongues **8**
Ears and noses **10**
Legs **12**
Feet...**14**
Tails...**16**
Amphibians with a difference...........**18**
Amphibian babies............................**20**
Totally amazing amphibian
    body parts! **22**
Glossary **23**
Find out more..................................**24**
Index **24**

Some words are shown in bold, **like this**. You can find out what they mean by looking in the glossary.

What is an amphibian?

Frogs, toads and newts are all amphibians.

Most amphibians start their lives in water. As they grow up, their bodies change. This is so they can also live on land.

Amphibians do not all look the same. Their bodies can be very different from each other.

Let's take a look at parts of their bodies.

Eyes

Some amphibians have very large eyes.

Frogs can't turn their heads. Their **bulging** eyes help them see all around them.

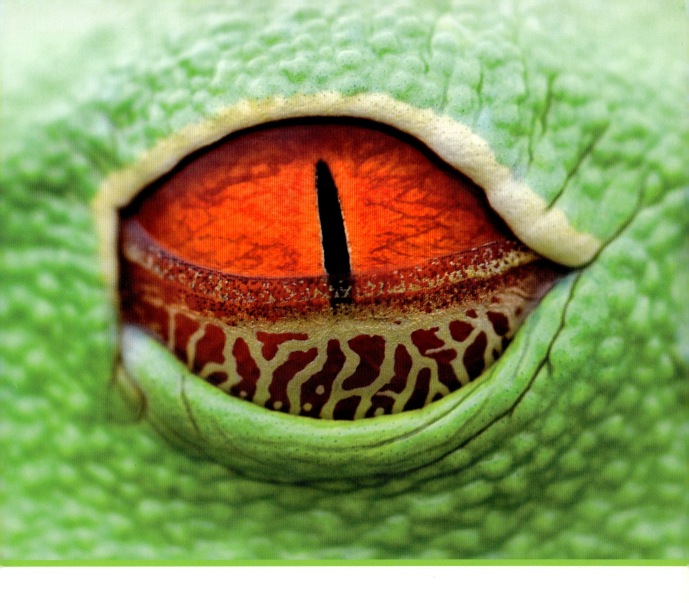

Frogs have two eyelids on each eye. One of the eyelids is see-through.

This eyelid helps the frog to protect its eyes while swimming under water.

Teeth and tongues

earthworm

Amphibians eat small animals and insects.

Frogs have teeth, but they can't chew. They use their teeth to grip their **prey**.

Many amphibians have powerful tongues.

This slingshot tongue salamander shoots out its tongue at high speed to catch insects.

Ears and noses

ear

Most amphibians have good hearing. They listen for **predators**.

Amphibians have ears behind their eyes.

Frogs and toads have noses on top of their heads.

This frog can hide in the water. It is waiting for a tasty insect to pass by.

Legs

Frogs have long and powerful back legs.

Their legs are good for swimming and jumping. This frog is leaping away from a **predator**.

Toads and salamanders have short back legs.

This European common toad mainly moves around by walking or crawling.

Feet

tree frog

Some amphibians, such as tree frogs, have sticky feet.

Sticky feet help them to climb up trees and rocks.

Frogs that live in water have webbed feet.

Webbed feet have skin between the toes. Webbed feet help animals to push through water.

Tails

This great crested newt is a type of salamander. Its long tail helps it swim well.

Frogs and toads start life with tails, but the tails disappear as they grow older.

This salamander can make its tail fall off. It does this to escape from **predators**.

A new tail will soon grow in its place.

Amphibians with a difference

Caecilians are a type of amphibian. They mainly live under ground.

Caecilians don't have legs. Their long, thin bodies are good for burrowing into the earth.

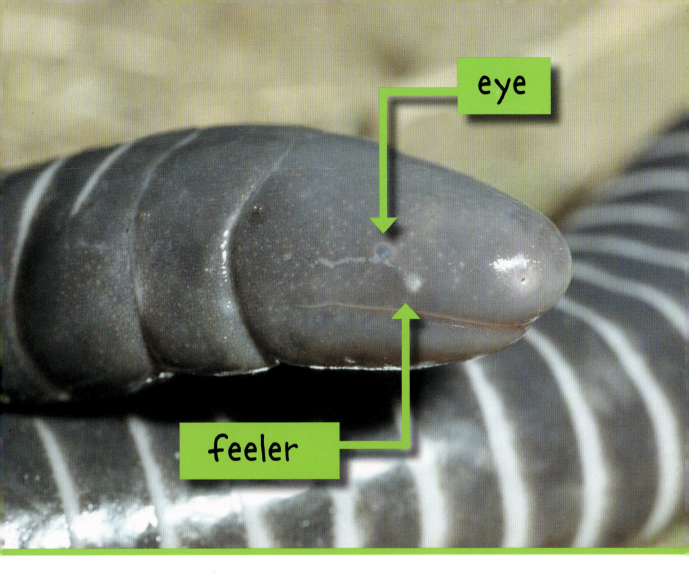

Caecilians have small eyes and no ears.

Instead, caecilians have tiny feelers on their heads to help them find **prey**.

Amphibian babies

Most amphibian babies look different from their parents. As they grow, they change.

Frog babies are called tadpoles. They hatch from eggs.

Tadpoles have long tails and no legs at first. They breathe through **gills** on the sides of their bodies.

As the tadpoles get bigger, their legs grow and their tails and gills disappear.

Totally amazing amphibian body parts!

The male North American bullfrog has a large pouch under its mouth. The bullfrog croaks to find a **mate**. Its pouch puffs up to make the croak louder.

The body of a Chinese giant salamander can grow to 1.8 metres (6 feet) long. That's as long as a sofa!

The Lake Titicaca frog has folds and flaps of skin all over its body. The flaps help the frog get enough **oxygen** from the water.

Glossary

bulging popping out

gills parts of the body that let animals breathe under water

mate partner of an animal. Male animals look for female mates.

oxygen gas that all animals need to live

predator animal that hunts other animals for food

prey animal that is hunted by another animal

Find out more

Books

Amphibians (Animal Classifications), Angela Royston (Raintree, 2015)

Life Story of a Frog (Animal Life Stories), Charlotte Guillain (Raintree, 2014)

Websites

Learn about some amazing amphibians at:
animals.nationalgeographic.com/animals/amphibians

Find wonderful photographs and watch videos all about amphibians at:
www.bbc.co.uk/nature/life/Amphibian#intro

Index

babies 20–21

eggs 20

gills 21, 23

jumping 12

predators 10, 12, 17, 23

prey 8, 19, 23

sticky feet 14

webbed feet 15